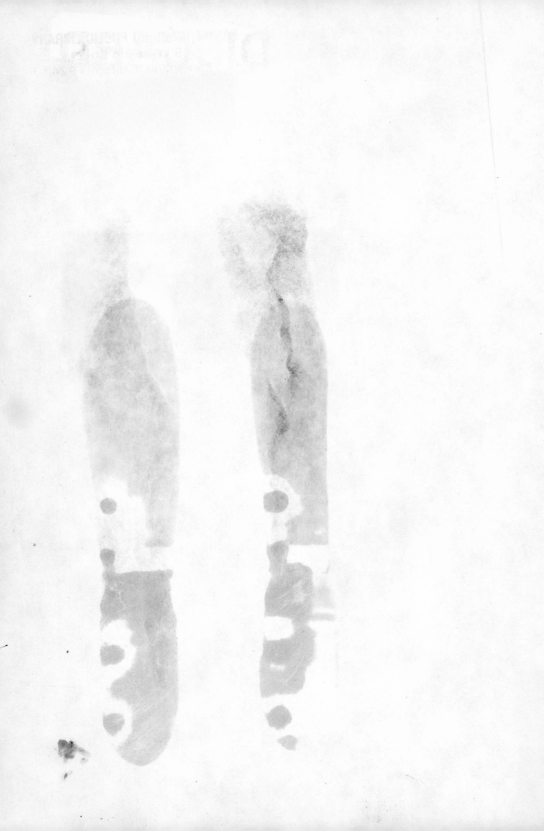

Lou Gehrig

PRIDE OF THE YANKEES

Lou Gehrig
PRIDE OF THE YANKEES

by Keith Brandt
illustrated by John Lawn

Troll Associates

Library of Congress Cataloging in Publication Data

Brandt, Keith, (date)
     Lou Gehrig, Pride of the Yankees.

     Summary: Describes the life of the great baseball
player, from his childhood as the only son of German
immigrants to his triumph as star of the New York
Yankees.
     1. Gehrig, Lou, 1903-1941—Juvenile literature.
2. Baseball players—United States—Biography—Juvenile
literature.   3. New York Yankees (Baseball team)—
Juvenile literature.   [1. Gehrig, Lou, 1903-1941.
2. Baseball players]   I. Lawn, John, ill.   II. Title.
GV865.G4B7   1986   796.357 '092 '4 [B] [92]   85-1075
ISBN 0-8167-0549-6 (lib. bdg.)
ISBN 0-8167-0550-X (pbk.)

Lou Gehrig

PRIDE OF THE YANKEES

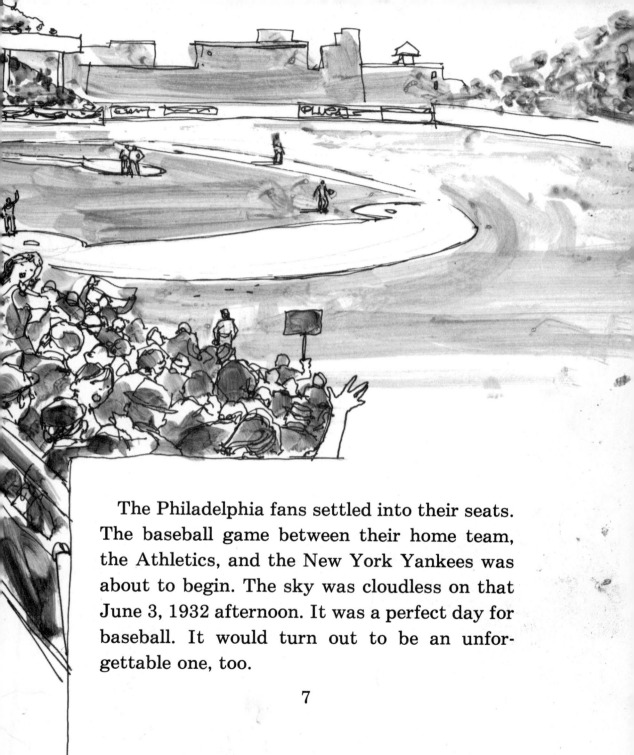

The Philadelphia fans settled into their seats.
The baseball game between their home team,
the Athletics, and the New York Yankees was
about to begin. The sky was cloudless on that
June 3, 1932 afternoon. It was a perfect day for
baseball. It would turn out to be an unfor-
gettable one, too.

The first Yankee batter of the game got on base. The next batter made an out, and the batter after that—the great Babe Ruth—struck out. This brought Lou Gehrig up to bat. The Philadelphia pitcher, George Earnshaw, wound up and threw the ball. Gehrig swung, there was a loud *smack*, and the baseball sailed far over the left-field fence. It was a home run. Now the Yankees led, 2–0.

The teams battled on. Every time Philadelphia tied the score or went ahead of the Yankees, Lou Gehrig came to bat. Each of those times, his hitting put the Yankees in front again. He hit his second home run of the game in the fourth inning, and his third home run in the fifth inning.

In the seventh inning, the first two Yankees to bat hit home runs. Philadelphia's manager, Connie Mack, decided to take Earnshaw out of the game and replace him with relief pitcher Roy Mahaffey. As Earnshaw approached the Philadelphia dugout, Manager Mack said, "Watch closely. I want you to see how Mahaffey pitches to Gehrig."

Earnshaw, Mack, both teams, and thousands of fans watched closely. Mahaffey reared back and threw his best pitch to Gehrig. Gehrig, in turn, did his best. He drove the ball over the right-field fence. Incredibly, it was his fourth home run of the game!

In the Philadelphia dugout, Earnshaw smiled at his manager and said, "I believe I see now, Mr. Mack. Mahaffey made him hit it to the other field, didn't he?" Connie Mack just shook his head. Lou Gehrig was as tough a hitter as *any* pitcher had ever faced.

11

Henry Louis Gehrig was born on June 19, 1903, in New York City. His parents, Heinrich and Christina Gehrig, were German immigrants who had come to America in search of a better life. They were hard-working, honest people, but they knew no English when they first arrived in New York. This made it difficult for them to find work, and to take part in the life around them.

Mr. Gehrig was trained in Germany as a leaf-hammerer. He knew how to hammer designs into metal sheets. It was a fine skill, and he earned good wages when there was work for him. But often there were no leaf-hammering jobs to be had. During those bad stretches, Mr. Gehrig earned money as a handyman, a butcher, or a janitor. Sometimes there was leaf-hammering work, but it required him to go to another city. Those months, while he was away in Chicago, Cleveland, or Detroit, were lonely times in the Gehrig house.

Much of the time, Mrs. Gehrig was the family breadwinner. She worked as a cook and house-keeper for wealthy families. She also made money by doing the laundry of other people. But in spite of the long hours of work she did for others, Mrs. Gehrig never failed to do her own family's washing, cooking, and sewing.

Before Lou was born, Mrs. Gehrig had given birth to two children. Both of them had died before they were a year old. When Lou proved to be a healthy baby, Mrs. Gehrig gave him all the love and attention she had saved up for years. She was determined that his life would be better than hers and her husband's. To accomplish this, Mrs. Gehrig was willing to work day and night.

15

The devotion of his mother was an important factor in Lou Gehrig's life. When he was a successful baseball player, receiving a high salary, he made sure that his mother and father shared his success. He bought them a fine home, and insisted that they stop working so they could enjoy their old age. It was his way of saying "Thank you!" for all their sacrifices during his childhood.

One of Lou's earliest memories was riding the trolley car with his mother. He wasn't old enough to go to school, so he went with Mrs. Gehrig to her jobs. While she cooked or cleaned house, the boy sat and played quietly in the kitchen. Then, at night, Lou helped his mother carry the laundry she would wash and iron at home.

Those first five years of Lou Gehrig's life did much to form his personality. As an adult, he was shy, quiet, and serious—just like that small boy who was with his mother all day.

Lou spent so much time with his mother that he had little chance to make friends. Even on Sunday, when he was free to play in the neighborhood, he was not able to talk to the other children. That was because Lou knew only a few words of English. His parents spoke in German all the time, and that was the language he learned. Not until Lou began attending public school, when he was five years old, did he start to learn English.

School made a big difference in Lou's life in many ways. Once he began to speak English, he made friends. He was still a quiet little boy, but he enjoyed playing with other children. Even before he could speak English well, Lou found a way to communicate with the other boys and girls—in sports.

19

Lou Gehrig was not a natural athlete. But he was strong, eager to learn, and ready to practice something until he got it right. When he began playing baseball, soon after he turned five years old, he was a chubby, awkward child. He didn't throw well, catch well, or run the bases well. Still, Lou was always asked to play in the school yard and in street games. That was because he was one of the best hitters in the neighborhood.

For Lou, doing well at baseball was important. He was teased about being clumsy and fat, about not speaking English well, and about his funny clothing. Lou's parents dressed him in the style they knew from Europe, which was different from the American style. When the other children poked fun at him, Lou was too quiet to answer back with words. He let his baseball abilities do the talking for him.

Mr. and Mrs. Gehrig were glad to see their child make friends. They heard Lou talk about baseball all the time, about the bats and balls and gloves the other kids used. After a while, they realized he didn't have any baseball equipment of his own. Lou never said anything, but it was clear what he wanted. His mother and father set out to make that Christmas of 1908 a special one for Lou.

The Gehrigs were too poor to buy a Christmas tree. But Mr. Gehrig found a small piece of an evergreen tree. The tree piece lay in the street, waiting for a garbage pickup, when Mr. Gehrig spotted it. He brought it home on Christmas Eve, and hid it in a closet.

After Lou went to bed, the Gehrigs set the little piece of tree on a table. They decorated it with walnuts and bits of ribbon. Under the tree they placed Lou's presents. There was a stocking filled with cookies, nuts, and an orange. Next to the stocking was a baseball glove. It did not cost a lot, but for the Gehrigs it was expensive.

The next morning, when Lou found his presents, he was overjoyed. The glove meant so much to him, because he knew how poor his parents were. It did not even matter that it was a right-handed catcher's mitt, and Lou was left-handed. The glove made him a real American baseball player. It was a Christmas morning he never forgot. When he was grown-up, he said that glove was the best present he ever received.

The winter Lou received his first glove seemed endless to him. Every night, he slept with the glove beside his pillow. He could barely wait until the weather was warm enough for the baseball games to start again. The arrival of spring 1909 was as exciting as any spring he spent in the major leagues.

In Lou's neighborhood, baseball games were played in the morning, before school began. The boys met in a vacant lot or the school yard, as soon as it grew light. Most of the children got up around five o'clock, gulped down breakfast, and raced out to play. The game continued until the school bell called them inside.

The children would have played after school, too, but most of them couldn't. As young as they were, Lou and his playmates had jobs or home chores to do after school.

It was normal for children to help their families in any way they could. Children might deliver packages, shovel snow, or work in a local store. Even those who did not have paying jobs had responsibilities. Apartments where the Gehrigs lived had stoves that burned coal or wood. The fuel for these stoves had to be carried upstairs, and the children were given this task. They also helped with the laundry, cooking, cleaning, taking care of younger brothers and sisters, and anything else that had to be done.

As hard as this life may sound, it could have been worse. At the beginning of the twentieth century, it was perfectly legal for children to work full time. They did not have to attend a single day of school. Lou and his friends knew they were better off than lots of others their age. They might have just a few years of education, but they wouldn't be illiterate.

Mrs. Gehrig wanted more than only a few years of education for Lou. She wanted him to go to high school and to have a good-paying, steady job one day. Mrs. Gehrig dreamed that her son would not be a laborer who did hard, physical work. She pictured him wearing a suit and a starched white shirt, just like the gentlemen for whom she worked as a housekeeper.

Though he was not a fast learner in school, Lou always earned good marks. That was because his mother saw to it that Lou studied. She insisted that he practice his penmanship over and over, so that each letter looked perfect. She made him do arithmetic until there wasn't a single mistake on the page. She showed her love for her son by encouraging him to set high goals and to be a person on whom others could depend.

Lou did not object to his mother's standards, because they were the same standards he set for himself. As an adult, Lou Gehrig did not allow illness, injury, or anything else to keep him out of a baseball game. It was part of his pride and personality to be steady and reliable, as well as a fine ballplayer. Lou Gehrig is best remembered for having played in 2,130 consecutive games—a baseball record. This dependability earned him the nickname, "The Iron Horse."

Lou's serious attitude began long before he entered the big leagues. For example, he never missed a day of school. Even when he had pneumonia in second grade, he wouldn't stay home. A perfect attendance record was important to him.

At school, Lou did as well in sports as he did in class work. By seventh grade, he was an outstanding shot-putter on the track team. He played running back and tackle on the football team. On the soccer field, he played different positions and enjoyed all of them. But once baseball season began, Lou put all other sports aside.

When Lou was in eighth grade, his father became very ill and could not work. It looked like Lou would have to get a full-time job, instead of going on to high school. But Mrs. Gehrig did not want her son to sacrifice his future. She took a job as cook-housekeeper for a fraternity house at Columbia University.

Mrs. Gehrig's job paid only enough to cover the family's basic needs. As a result, she continued to take in laundry and to clean other people's houses. Lou helped out, too, by working at the fraternity house on weekends. Then, when Mr. Gehrig was better, he became the janitor at the fraternity house. Because of this work, Lou felt a loyalty to Columbia University. For years before he was a student there, the school meant a lot to him.

In the fall of 1917, Lou entered the High School of Commerce. There, he became a baseball star. A schoolmate remembered, "He came to school by subway, took two steps at a time going up and down stairs, seldom wore a vest or topcoat in cold weather, and had a terrific appetite. What made us suddenly realize at Commerce that Lou was different from other varsity ballplayers was a home run that he hit in an intercity game against Lane Tech of Chicago at Wrigley Field."

That Wrigley Field game, which became part of the Lou Gehrig legend, took place on June 28, 1920. Lou had just turned seventeen, and was about to be graduated from high school. His powerful hitting had carried Commerce High to the New York City championship and earned them the invitation to Chicago. But Lou almost did not get to make the trip.

The teen-ager had never been outside New York City. Lou's parents felt he was not ready for an overnight train journey by himself. Besides, they couldn't afford to pay his expenses. The Commerce High coach, Harry Kane, assured the Gehrigs that Lou would be safe. He would watch the boy, day and night. Furthermore, the school was paying for everything. So, Lou took his first long-distance train ride. He would log thousands of miles on trains during his major-league career, but this was the trip he remembered best.

In the game between Commerce and Lane, Lou's big moment came in the ninth inning. Commerce was ahead, but Lane had its best hitters coming up in the second half of the inning. Commerce, however, had three men on base, and the chance to build a large lead. Gehrig, who hadn't recorded a hit all day, was due to bat. Nervously, he asked Coach Kane, "What should I do?"

With a smile, Kane answered, "Go and hit one

out of the park." The way Lou was hitting that
day, Kane really did not expect any such thing
to happen.

Lou said, "Yes, sir," went to the plate, and
swung at the first pitch. The crowd cheered as
the ball soared far over the right-field fence. It
was a grand-slam homer—a four-run hit blasted
with the force of a major leaguer.

The next day, the New York *Daily News* printed Lou's picture, with this line: "Louis Gehrig, Commerce slugger, the New York lad known as the Babe Ruth of the high schools." It thrilled Lou to see his picture and name in the newspaper.

The Gehrigs were proud of their boy, but even happier when he entered Columbia University. There, he studied engineering, played football, soccer, and, of course, baseball. Lou loved playing sports, but he had no intention of making a career as an athlete. Then trouble came. When Lou finished his sophomore year at Columbia, his father became seriously ill again. This changed the course of Lou's life.

Lou could not afford to stay in college. His family needed whatever money he could earn. What's more, Mr. Gehrig had to have an operation, and that would be expensive. Lou began to think about becoming a professional baseball player.

Since his high-school days, Lou had been watched by scouts for a number of major-league teams. But whenever they had approached him, he had turned down their offers. Now he let it be known that he was interested in talking to them. As soon as the word got out, the scouts came to see him.

The best offer came from the New York Yankees, who were willing to pay Lou $1,500 for signing a contract. That was a lot of money in those days. It would pay for Mr. Gehrig's operation, and take care of the family while he recuperated. This was what Lou wanted, and he became a Yankee in June 1923. He was twenty years old.

Mr. Gehrig's operation was a success. Lou's beginning as a major leaguer, however, was not so successful. He could hit well, but the rest of his baseball skills needed sharpening. Two years in the minor leagues took care of that. Then, in 1925, Lou rejoined the Yankees. On June 1 of that year, he was sent into a game as a pinch hitter.

From that day, until May 2, 1939, Lou Gehrig never missed playing in a game. During those fourteen seasons with the Yankees, he became one of America's sports idols. Along with Babe Ruth, Gehrig led the New York Yankees through their Golden Era. In fact, the Yankees

of 1927 are called by many, "the greatest team in baseball history."

Lou set many records in his career. He hit a record total of twenty-three grand-slam home runs. He led the American League four times in runs scored, five times in home runs, and was voted the league's Most Valuable Player four times. He was one of the greatest hitters of all time.

By 1938, baseball's "Iron Horse" was beginning to slow down. Some days his hitting was as superb as ever. Yet on other days he could barely hit the ball. At first, he ignored these batting slumps. But after a while, it was clear that something was wrong.

Gehrig started the 1939 season with the hope that he would be back in top form. Instead, he was worse than ever. A medical examination showed the reason. Lou had a disease that slowly destroys the nervous system. He was told he had a short time to live, and that the condition could not be cured.

When Lou Gehrig retired from baseball in May 1939, the sports world was stunned. It did not seem possible that this strong young man, who looked as if he could play forever, was dying. Sadly, it was true, and people rushed to show him their respect and admiration. Lou did not have to wait to be voted into the Baseball Hall of Fame. The waiting rule was set aside, and he was unanimously voted in that same year.

On July 4, 1939, the Yankees retired his uniform, number 4, forever. The ceremonies took place at Yankee Stadium, on Lou Gehrig Appreciation Day. Between the first and second games of a double-header, a microphone was set up at home plate. Many people paid tribute to Lou Gehrig, the man called the "Pride of the Yankees." There was his old teammate, Babe Ruth; New York City's Mayor Fiorello LaGuardia; players from the past and present; sportswriters; and baseball officials.

Then, as more than seventy-thousand people listened, Lou Gehrig said with deep feeling, "Fans, for the past two weeks you have been reading about a bad break I got. Yet today I consider myself the luckiest man on the face of the earth. I have been in ballparks for seventeen years, and have never received anything but kindness and encouragement from you fans.... So I close in saying that I might have had a tough break; but I have an awful lot to live for."

Two years later, on June 2, 1941, Lou Gehrig died. It was exactly sixteen years from the day he began his unbroken streak of consecutive baseball games. "The Iron Horse" was now a part of sports history.